Combining inspirational poetry, en[...] model prayers to aid readers in a triumphant Christian life, *The Call to Peace, Clarity, and Purpose*, by Ruby Heaton, offers a deeper path with God. As *Deep Calls unto Deep*, you'll find the author's poetry rich with free verse; the Creator's positive words of power in the prose; and the creativity to reflect, pray, plan, grow, and achieve.

Take a moment to ponder . . . If you desire purpose and power as life happens, this book is for you!

Dr. Edna Ellison, Author and Speaker

Spartanburg, South Carolina

Having trained Christian speakers and writers for most of my adult life, I am always excited when one of my students publishes his or her first book. Ruby Heaton's new book The Call, is a thought-provoking cross between a typical personal-growth book, a devotional, and a collection of poetry. It combines Ruby's original poems with scripture, prayers and photography with gentle instruction- all thematically arranged. It would be effective used on a daily basis and/or as needs arise in the readers personal life.

Marita Littauer, President, CLASServices Inc.

Speaker, Author of 20 books

The Mountaintops and Valleys of Life...

I stood on the mountaintops

and thought life was beautiful,

Until I fell into the valleys.

I saw light and beauty all around,

Until I got lost in a dark tunnel.

I had many victories

And thought I had this life all figured out,

Until I lost everything,

and was side-swept out to sea.

I thought I knew who I was,

Who the world had made me,

Until I found Him,

And discovered my way out of the valleys,

the dark tunnel, and the sea,

And discovered my Destiny.

Your word is a lamp to my feet, and a light to my path (Psalm 119:105NKJV)

The Call to Peace, Clarity, and Purpose

Deep Calls unto Deep

By Ruby Heaton

The Call to Peace, Clarity, and Purpose   Deep Calls unto Deep

Printed in the United States of America by Heaton Publishing

www.RubyHeaton.com

Independently Published

ISBN 978-1-7362278-0-0

Ruby Heaton

Table Contents

Acknowledgement

Meet Me on the Mountaintops

To you who have journeyed by my side through the valleys.

You who have encouraged me,

Laughed with me,

And cried with me,

Given me your ear,

Your hand,

And your heart,

I will prepare a place for you on my mountaintops.

Introduction

I have always loved writing and I journal quite a bit. I journal when I am happy, when I discover something new, when I study the Bible, when I find myself searching, and when I cry out to God for help or direction. I find writing can bring clarity.

This collection is a mixture of writing that I posted on blogs, Church publications, and Face Book, along with some I felt led to write as I worked on the book. Many of these came from the numerous trials I endured, from the things I witnessed, and from the counsel I have given. The writings can stand alone, but many of them flow well together and expound on a point, so I grouped them into chapters.

I have been told that some of my writings sound like Psalms, that they bring comfort and wisdom. Due to all the positive comments, I got the idea to put some into a book. I share my feelings, my discoveries, my revelations, and thoughts to inspire you. I added questions to help you reflect, and action steps to get you moving in a positive direction to help improve your life. My prayer is that I can bless you and encourage you to grow stronger in your walk so that you are inspired to draw closer to God and to live the life that you were created to live. I hope and pray these words inspire you to reach a place of peace, healing, and purpose.

You can read this book on your own, with a friend, or use it with several friends as a group study. Chapter 12 has weekly ideas that you can start doing now.

If you do not have God in your life, you can ask Him to come in. You have to take the first step and believe. I know it may be hard. Here is what you can ask: "God, if you are real, please come into my life, show me who you are and help my unbelief." You have so much to gain; what do you have to lose?

You can pray this simple prayer:

Jesus, come into my heart. Forgive me for all my sins and help me to forgive anyone who has hurt me. Cleanse me and deliver me and heal my mind, body, and emotions. Write my name in the Book of Life. Give me the Holy Spirit, fill me with your wisdom, teach me your ways, and give me favor. In Jesus' name I ask,

Amen.

God, I come into agreement with the person who has just said

this prayer. Please help them to know you are real. Let them feel

your love and comfort them. Send your angels to surround them

and lead them. Place a hedge of protection around them and

provide for all their needs. Speak to their heart as they read this

book, allow it to minister to them in profound ways.

God, I ask you in Jesus' name let it be so,

Your daughter Ruby

He's My Everything

He is like my warm cup of cocoa on a snowy day,

He is like my blanket on a cold beach,

He is like an umbrella in the blazing sun,

He is like my light in a dark world,

He is like my ladder when I fall short,

He is like my sunshine when I'm sad,

He gives hope when I want to give up.

Insight

To do anything great you must take a chance...

Having character and morals and doing noble things…

will come at a cost,

Truly caring for a cause or a person…

will require a great deal of your time and energy,

Loving something or someone…

will humble you and change you completely.

Chapter 1

Storms and Valleys

Sometimes the best changes emerge with time and trials.

They occur from within,

and they are able to transform your world...

Call them what you want, storms, valleys, or trials, we all find ourselves going through them no matter how hard we may try to avoid them. I know; I have made the journey far more times than I thought was fair. But who am I to decide what is fair?

Some of the knowledge I gained through the hardship and pain I have endured helped launch me into ministry and teaching at churches, homes, women's shelters, and other locations. Many of the things I have learned from my experiences help me in assisting the people who come to me for help, because I am able to relate to many of their feelings, fears, concerns, and actions.

I have been humbled and changed by the weight of all my trials. They changed the way I view situations, trials, people, and

God. I have learned a lot of what works and what doesn't. I do not have all the answers and my life is not perfect, but I serve a perfect God who does have all the answers. I have learned how to pray and seek His answers for my situations. When I run ahead of Him and things get messy, I change direction and allow God to correct me.

The Word tells us that we are to continually grow. Trials are definitely a way to grow. I find it is best to learn all you can before the next one arrives. In fact, learning from our trials, or the trials of others, can help us avoid some. I remember a joke that went something like this, "Some people live life as a warning to other people of what not to do." We probably all know someone like that or have heard about them. People that make one mistake after another and never seem to realize that they cause a lot of their own problems by making bad choices. In truth, we have all probably been that warning at some point in our lives because we have all made mistakes. When I reflected on my past, I realized I made some poor choices and I could have avoided some things I had to endure. I have yet to meet a perfect person and I know you have not met one because the Word tells us no one is perfect. We are not called to be perfect, but we are expected to learn and improve.

As you read, be real with yourself and write down things you remember-- such as the times when you suffered, the lessons you learned, the foolish things you did or said, and any insights you may get. Your insights are the most important things. Their purpose is for you to see your truth, so you do not have to go in circles repeating the same trials.

Prayer:

God, help us to avoid all the trials we possibly can. Lead us through the trials we must go through quickly and with as little damage as possible. Help us to learn what we must, to reflect and grow, and to retain and share that wisdom with others so they will not have to suffer as we did. In Jesus' name we ask. Amen.

God, I lift up everyone going through a trial and ask that your hand be upon them. God, give them favor, wisdom, clarity, and strength to do what they must. Help them to find peace, insight, direction and comfort in reading these words. In Jesus' name I

ask. Amen.

My brethren, count it all joy when you fall into various trials,

knowing that the testing of your faith produces patience. But let

patience have its perfect work, that you may be perfect and

complete, lacking nothing. (James 1:2-4 NKJV)

The Dark Nights of the Soul

The stretching and the breaking,

The bruising and the crushing,

The pulling and the pushing,

Wondering and analyzing,

On the path and then off again,

Lost and all alone, going in circles,

Grasping and almost reaching, crying out in anguish,

Inquiring, demanding and getting no response.

What a job this soul searching!

Oh, the battles that rage...

in the mixed emotions in the mind,

So long and lonely,

So deep and weary,

So hard and exhausting,

The dark nights of the soul cause us to look deep

within the places we refused to go on our own,

To examine our motives, our beliefs and our attitudes,

and to make the necessary changes.

There is much pain and loss on this journey of discovery,

But far more is gained.

The Battle Within

Sometimes I wonder...

Why it can't all be so simple?

Why all the confusion?

Why all the drama and the pain?

Why the waiting and the mystery?

Why the chasing as if after the wind?

Why all the unanswered questions?

Why all the doubts?

Why? Why, God, why?

Then the answer comes,

I know deep within…

With confusion I am forced to find clarity and truth,

With pain comes growth and then joy,

The waiting causes me to search within and without.

The mystery leads me to God's Word and to God,

The doubts cause me to question my beliefs,

And they cause me to find out who I truly am

and what I really believe,

Causing my footing to be far more secure,

So that I am prepared for the next battle …within.

Trials, Storms, and Pain

There comes a point in time,

When we have to face reality,

Truth hits us, there is no running,

And we realize that we will have to endure trials and pain.

The good with the bad,

The joy with the pain,

Near perfection with imperfection,

Clarity with confusion,

The flip side of the coin always turns up.

What is the point, the purpose, the reason?

The trials stretch and mold us,

They grow and transform us,

They teach us many things...

Who we can really trust,

What we are capable of,

Our strengths and weaknesses,

What we need to work on,

What we believe and do not really believe...

Who we really are,

And who God is.

Loss

When we lose someone close,

The pain is deep, long, and crushing at times,

I know this loss because I have lost many loved ones…

My father, relatives, friends, and my spiritual mother.

When my heart grieves for them there are moments…

when their presence is almost tangible,

I hear their words,

I see a picture of them in my mind,

And the memories come.

I remember the silly things we said or did,

The adventures we shared.

I hear their laughter,

And I share a laugh with them again.

All that they have brought into my life…

The wisdom, the laughter, the peace, and the love,

It all still exists,

In this I am comforted,

It brings peace to my soul.

The Narrow Road

You will come to many crossroads

on your journey called life,

Some will cause minor change,

Some will cause major change,

Take time to select the best path

because many paths will have no turning back.

The roads you travel on will be lonely at times,

They may require you to be brave and strong,

No one will want to follow some of the places you go to.

There are paths where people will not be able to keep up with the

pace or handle the altitude,

Sometimes there will be pruning and humbling taking place,

Other times you will need the solitude to listen, reflect, grow, and

achieve,

On some roads you will leave a trail of tears,

Others will echo with your laughter.

You help determine the detours, the destination and what the

roads have in store for you,

So, pray hard and choose wisely.

I will instruct you and teach you in the way you should go; I will

guide you with my eye. (Psalm 32:8 NKJV)

Prayer:

God, help me and guide me as I come to my crossroads. Fill me with the wisdom to choose correctly. Strengthen me so I am able to stand by my choices when temptations and loneliness try to overtake me. Give me a sound mind so I do not listen when the enemy tries to lie to me or confuse me. Fill me with your peace, and help me to adjust and let go of the things and people I must leave behind.

Give me supernatural strength and joy for the journey and help me to keep my focus on you, God, on love, on the good things that really matter, and on the steps, I need to take to accomplish my goals. In Jesus' name I ask. Amen.

"These things I have spoken to you, that in me you may have peace. In the world you will have tribulation; but be of good cheer, I have overcome the world." (John 16:33 NKJV)
When your terror comes like a storm, And your destruction comes like a whirlwind, When distress and anguish come upon you. (Proverbs 1:27 NKJV)

I will instruct you and teach you in the way you should go; I will guide you with my eye. (Psalm 32:8 NKJV)

He restores my soul; He leads me in the paths of righteousness For His name's sake. Yea, though I walk through the valley of the shadow of death, I will fear no evil; For you are with me; your rod and your staff, they comfort me. (Psalm 23:3-4NKJV)

Chapter 2

Deep Calls unto Deep

I hear the call of the wind... I hear the lark's sweet songs ...

I hear the sound of a distant rain... I hear the call of nature...

I have read that nature itself speaks of God and if we stay silent the trees and rocks will cry out. Around the world and in remote villages, people tell stories of a great flood and a man like Noah and other similar biblical stories and they talk about God encounters. God is always calling out to us.

Deep calls unto deep at the noise of your waterfalls; All your waves and billows have gone over me. (Psalm 42:7 NKJV)

But He answered and said to them, "I tell you that if these should keep silent, the stones would immediately cry out." (Luke 19:40 NKJV)

God calls all of us even if we do not want to listen. No one can hide and no one can outrun Him. Think back to the times you felt God was calling you or speaking to you about something He wanted you to do. Was it a dream, a thought, words you heard or kept on hearing from friends, strangers, or a sermon? Something you read that stood out, or a car radio that could only get reception from a Christian station? I have had all of these things happen to me. I usually get the same message in three different ways when God is telling me something. Many people have told me they have had similar experiences.

How can you not hear God? He gives us a sunrise every morning, He paints beautiful sunsets at night, and He sends the wind to whisper to us. He is all around, speaking through all His handiwork. What have you sensed or felt God saying to you?

God desires to save us, to heal us, to teach us, and to empower us because He loves us. He beckons us to trust Him, to follow Him, to rise up and grow, to be empowered for the battle and to be victorious.

(Psalm 139:7-12 NKJV) Tells us that we cannot hide from God.

Where can I go from your spirit? Or where can I flee from your presence? If I ascend into heaven, you are there; If I make my bed in hell, behold, you are there. If I take the wings of the morning, And dwell in the uttermost parts of the sea, Even there your hand shall lead me, And your right hand shall hold me. If I say, "Surely the darkness shall fall on me," Even the night shall be light about me; Indeed, the darkness shall not hide from you, But the night shines as the day; The darkness and the light are both alike to you.

(Psalm 144:1 NKJV) Tells us that not only is God our strength, He also teaches us how to fight and win like He did for David. We need only ask, listen and learn.

A Psalm of David. Blessed be the Lord my Rock, Who trains my hands for war, And my fingers for battle—

The Call...

Like a gentle whisper on the wind,

Or a loud thunder,

Soft yet mighty,

Simple yet profound.

So many facets,

So many secrets to discover,

Exciting,

Enlightening,

Amazing,

More than we can imagine or fathom,

He calls us,

He beckons for us to come closer.

Can you not hear?

Do you not sense Him close by?

Are you not able to feel His presence surrounding you?

Can You Hear Him?

Freedom writers,

Risk takers,

Mountain movers,

Earth shakers,

Vessels,

Instruments,

Mouthpieces,

Saints,

Children of the King,

Ambassadors,

Royal Priesthood,

Warriors,

Mighty men of God,

Holy nation.

God is calling out to you,

Listen and Arise!

Holy, Holy, Holy God.

Let the rain fall,

and the rivers flow,

Empower Your faithful ones to war in the spirit

and in the heavens.

The Measure of a Man

When you look at a man…

His beliefs,

His values,

His actions and his fruit,

They speak volumes...

Even when he is silent...

You Are Light

God says,

You are light,

A reflection of Me,

You're My children,

My vessels,

My royal priesthood,

My warriors,

My intercessors,

My battle-axes.

You're My voices in a dead and lost world.

You carry My anointing,

My love,

My power,

And my wisdom.

You can do great things in my name,

Because I created you to move the immovable,

To reach the unreachable,

To shake up the stagnant,

To wake up the dead,

To enlighten the deaf and dumb,

And to set the captives free.

Stay connected to me, for the time to move is now!

Many Are Called

Many are called...

Few really answer the call of Jesus.

We do things our own way

and on our own terms.

Many are called...

We fear,

We draw back,

We doubt.

Many are called...

Some ignore him,

Some put him on hold,

Some are scared to answer,

Some are hurt, or angry.

Many are called...

Some are too immersed in the world

and in its systems,

Some are too fleshly,

Some refuse to turn from their sinful ways.

Many are called...

Some aren't strong enough,

Some aren't bold enough,

Some aren't wise enough,

Some have no backbone.

Many are called...

All are able to answer the call.

Do you hear Him?

Rise up and arm yourself!

Get in line with the Word,

And say: Yes, Lord, here I am,

Send me.

The Fight

Don't contend with man,

Fight with the enemy of your soul

so you can lead men.

God is Calling His Children to a Closer Walk

It's about relationship,

Getting close to God,

Learning how to hear His voice,

And understanding His ways,

And staying connected.

Like the vine, He is our life source.

It's about knowing who God is,

Who we are,

and our place and calling.

It's about learning how to find our balance,

Learning self-control,

And learning to walk in our full authority,

With wisdom and power.

It's about running our best race,

It's about doing it all in the love of God.

Chapter 3

Rise Up

Arise, ascend at His call... He trains our hands

and minds for battle...

God expects us to rise up a little higher daily. To study His Word and get off the baby food. We are to worship God, be thankful in all things and keep a good attitude. Stay in faith. No murmuring and complaining. Repent when we sin, stay humble, and be forgiving and merciful, as God is with us. God even warns us if we do not forgive, He will not forgive us. Furthermore, we will be outside of His covering and we run the risk of bringing illnesses upon ourselves by our own anger or hate. We are to stay alert, be wise, run from temptation, and be prepared for the enemy who always roams around like a wild lion waiting for an open door.

We have to dust ourselves off and get back up when we fall, and try again. It is sometimes extremely hard. I find it best to get back to the basics. Pray, fast, praise God, and worship Him. Say what you are thankful for. Call some encouraging friends and share some laughter if possible, watch a funny movie, get a little sun daily, exercise, eat well and sleep well.

We are told to help our brothers, pray for them, encourage them, love them, and stay united. We must keep moving forward, be persistent, tenacious, and keep advancing.

Jesus said to Him, "'You shall love the Lord your God with all your heart, with all your soul, and with all your mind.' This is the first and great commandment. 'And the second is like it: 'You shall love your neighbor as yourself.' On these two commandments hang all the Law and the Prophets."
(Matt.22:37-40 NKJV)

Doors

There are many doors we will walk through,

Many roads we will travel,

Many friends we will make.

There are things we will leave behind,

Places we will leave behind,

And people we will leave behind.

There are attitudes we will have to adjust,

and behaviors we will have to break.

We will have to learn, grow, bend and change,

and fine-tune ourselves to survive.

We decide if we stay down when we fall

or we get back up, dust ourselves off,

and walk through another door.

Success

The first steps towards a successful life

are when we refuse to be held captive by old mindsets,

by circumstances,

by traditions,

by habits,

by people,

and by our past.

The second step is when we choose to follow God's principles

and our heart is conformed to His.

Rise Up and Move On

Sometimes when things fall apart or end,

we can seem to come apart or unravel,

we get trapped and are unaware, or fear holds us.

Think of what is lost by not moving on--

The chance at happiness that escapes you,

The people you never meet or get close to,

The experiences you never have,

The places you never travel to,

The joy you never feel.

Why?

Because you were once hurt,

now you refuse to really live.

You put yourself in your own man-made coffin of fear and

distrust.

What a sad and lonely place to be in!

Why not rise up and look to God the miracle-maker?

Ask Him to help you out of that desolate place

and take a shot at happiness?

Go for It!

We don't know all that God has placed within us

until we fully trust God.

When we fully trust God,

He'll give us the boldness…

to get out of the safety of the boat,

So we can take that first step,

and do some water-walking.

Get Back Up

There is no perfection,

Sometimes our ideas get smashed

and we get hurt,

But there is always a tomorrow.

With tomorrow comes a chance to get back up

and make our lives better.

No more looking back,

No more regrets,

No more what if's.

Take what you have learned and add to it.

 Move on,

Make some new plans,

Set some new goals.

Learn to dream again and go for your dreams...

The Word

Get the word in you,

and allow the word to operate in you.

So you are led by the word,

Taught by the word,

Encouraged by the word,

Built up by the word,

Get discernment by the word,

Are strengthened by the word,

And get solid footing on the word.

So you can walk in the power and authority

of the one who gave you the word.

"In the beginning was the Word, and the Word was with God,

and the Word was God" (John 1:1 KJV)

But Jesus answer him, saying, "It is written, Man shall not live

by bread alone, but by every word of God.'" (Luke 4:4 NKJV)

Life

Life is many things,

Exciting,

Challenging,

Interesting,

Difficult,

A mystery,

Rewarding,

Confusing,

A blessing,

And full of options.

In the end, it's what you make of it,

How you interpret it,

What you believe,

How you respond to it,

What you accept, reject, and create.

Believe you're able,

Believe you're worthy,

And create the best life you can!

Power to Create

God has told us that when we declare a thing, so shall it be. He said we are to guard our words because the tongue has the power to create, build up, or tear down.

This means that, positive or negative, you will have what you say and what you believe. God has said it in his word that as a man thinks so he is. If you think you can, you can. If you think you cannot, then you cannot. If you say, "I can't _____, it's too difficult", "I don't have the time", or "I can't afford that", your mind will believe what you say. Your mind will find a way to self-sabotage the thing you said you could not do. Your negative words spoke death over the situation.

If you speak positively and say, "I will do that in three months", your mind will act on your words and you will push yourself to do what you believe you can do. You will set goals, do research, and make phone calls for advice or help. Your mind will find a way to get it done.

I have seen this principle at work in my life and in the lives of my friends, family, and acquaintances. If you really want something and you believe it can happen, you will gravitate to it and find a way to attain it. The mind is amazing. It has the capability to imagine and create like our Creator. Once you realize this, so many doors can open for you.

You must remember to speak positive things over your family, your friends, and yourself. God has placed gifts in each one of us. He has said He came to give us life more abundantly. You must encourage yourself and others with positive words to step into the giftings and to have that abundant life. You can say things like, "I will", "I can do all things with God", "You are so smart I believe you can do that", or "I will pray for God to help you accomplish that". Remember to speak what you want to happen and do not speak any negative words, because they can hinder or kill any progress.

Prayer:

God, help me to speak what you would have me speak. Remind me to use words to build up and edify and not tear down so that I can encourage and help to create good outcomes. Help me to have self-control to refrain from saying the words I should not speak.

God, allow me to see myself through your eyes so I can become who you created me to be. Strengthen and empower my mind to believe everything you have for me to do and attain. Help me to build up, love, and encourage others so they can become who you created them to be and so they can attain all you have for them. In Jesus' name I ask you, God, let it be so. Amen.

Death and life are in the power of the tongue, And those who love it will eat its fruit. (Proverbs 18:21 NKJV)

There is one who speaks like the piercings of a sword, But the tongue of the wise promotes health. (Proverbs 12:18 NKJV)

Chapter 4

Self-Check

It is in the quiet moments of careful reflection

where the truth becomes evident and reality undeniable.

-Allison Heaton

God has told me to keep it simple and real. With that in mind, here are some truths to reflect on. We are told in the Word to work out our own salvation. That means we must look at ourselves and face our truths. Sometimes we may be blind or in denial, so we fail to see that we are off the mark. The older and wiser we get, the more we realize how imperfect we are. After continuing in the same negative patterns of behavior and making a mess of things or hurting our relationships, we are forced to see the truth and realize that we need to work on ourselves.

Self-improvement and discipline are very hard work. But we are the ones who benefit the most from being the best we can be.

We will have a better quality of life from good communication, great relationships, good health, and a better job. So why not take that self-check Jesus told us to do?

Search me, oh God, and know my heart; try me, and know my anxieties; And see if there is any wicked way in me, and lead me in the way everlasting. (Psalm 139:23-24 NKJV)

Prayer:

God, help me to take an honest look at myself. Show me what I need to correct or adjust. I am tired of making so many mistakes and going in circles. I want the best you have for me. Help me, Lord, in Jesus' name I ask. Amen.

Denial

Denial is a very hard place to escape,

because sometimes our hearts have to break,

our dreams have to die,

our lives must change,

Every comfort

and false security is stripped away.

Illusions of what is

and what could be

are pulverized,

As reality sets in and overrides

all the layers of denial.

Where Have We Robbed You, God?

Some in tithes and offerings,

Some in worship and praise,

Some in lack of time with me in my Word and in prayer.

Some in your lack of testimony,

Some in not focusing on me and in my promises,

Some in your lack of trust in me, my ways, and in my power.

Some in not training up your little ones to love and believe in me,

Some in not putting your hope in me and coming to me for

everything,

Some in your lack of deep love,

Some in not letting me be God in your life.

Ask yourself, where have I robbed God?

The Flesh in Me

The flesh in me

wants justice or revenge,

The God in me cries out forgive.

The flesh in me wants to do things the easy way of the world,

The God in me says follow, obey, and surrender.

The flesh in me doubts,

The God in me believes.

The flesh in me cowers in fear,

The God in me rises up like a lion.

I must finish crucifying the flesh.

Who Are You Making Your God?

We look to someone,

Run to someone,

Follow someone,

Cherish someone.

We give someone first place in our mind

 through desire, love, lust, or fear.

We give them our time, thoughts, and finances,

We may even let them control us,

We all make someone our God.

If not a person, then perhaps a thing,

Like food, money, status, lust, alcohol, or drugs.

Whom have you made your God?

Some People

Some people go through storms

and come out stronger.

Some people go through storms

and come out a soggy mess.

Some people go through tribulations

and come out wiser.

Some people go through tribulations

and lose their head.

Some people suffer abuse

and rise above it...

They grow... and forgive...

and they learn to love even more.

Some people suffer abuse and grow bitter, hard and unforgiving.

They can't love…

because they don't know how to love

They can't get past the hate.

"And whenever you stand praying, if you have anything against anyone, forgive him, that your Father in heaven may also forgive you your trespasses. But if you do not forgive, neither will your Father in heaven forgive your trespasses." (Mark 11:25-26 NKJV)

If it is possible, as much as it depends on you, live peaceably with all men. Beloved, do not avenge yourselves, but rather give place to wrath; for it is written, "Vengeance is Mine, I will repay," says the Lord. Therefore "if your enemy is hungry, feed him; If he is thirsty, give him a drink; For in so doing you will heap coals of fire on his head." Do not overcome evil by evil, but overcome evil with good. (Romans 12:18-21NKJV)

Prayer:

God, it's so hard to let go and forgive when I have been hurt, lied to, attacked, and betrayed. I need your help, Lord. Help me to do as you instruct. I know your ways work better than mine could ever work; please help me to walk in them. I give you my pain, anger, hate, and hurt, trusting that you will heal me and help me to rise above it all so I can find my power and joy again. I give you everyone who has hurt me, Lord God; you deal with them as you see fit. I forgive them with your help. Let it be a complete release from my hand, head, and heart to yours. In Jesus' name I ask you, God, let it be so. Amen.

The Lost

There are so many searching,

So many confused,

So many hurting,

So many broken,

So many lost.

So many hungry,

So many thirsty,

For truth...

For answers...

For breakthrough...

For miracles...

For provision,

And for you, oh Lord...

Yet they do not even know.

So they run back and forth

to all the wrong places

until they trip, stumble and fall.

Or they are hurt, confused, broken,

and depressed... ready to give up on life.

God, help them to find you.

Playing with Fire

Sin and temptation are interesting things.

Only the fool who says there is no God

thinks he can play with temptation

and not get burned.

The rest of us know better,

Yet still we play and fall at times.

Just knowing saves us from nothing.

It is in doing what God has told us to do

that we find wisdom, strength, and victory.

Reckless

The reckless heart,

Goes where it wants,

Does whatever it wants,

Answers to no one,

Has no obligations,

Belongs to no one.

The reckless soul

Has no connections,

No real destination,

No solid dreams or future.

He has no peace and no plan.

What a high price to pay

to be wild, irresponsible, and reckless.

Prayer:

God, I have been all of these at one time or another, lost, reckless, and the fool. God, I am one of the hurting, the walking wounded. I am overwhelmed and confused. I feel as if I have a heavy weight upon me at times. I do what I know I should not do. I cannot seem to help myself. Lord, please fill me with wisdom and the power to get control over my flesh so that I can contain my emotions. I must learn to rule my body so my emotions do not make a mess of my life. You say we are to be led by faith, wisdom, your spirit, and your truth, and not by our sight or our feelings.

Help me to walk in your ways allow me to find you, Lord. Reach out to me. Send your ministering angels to direct me on where to go, what to do and say or not say, and who to trust. Lord, direct my path daily. God, help me to see the truth. Remove any obstacles that are keeping me from finding you and your love and healing. Give me your peace and joy. In Jesus' name I ask. Amen.

Walls

There are so many walls,

There are walls between neighbors,

Walls between cultures,

Walls between age groups,

And walls between Christians,

There are walls between nations,

Walls between economic levels,

Walls between husbands and wives,

Walls between friends,

And Walls between us and God.

We put up walls both visible and invisible

for so many reasons.

Walls to separate, divide, and protect us,

Walls to hide our fears, insecurities, feelings and failings,

Walls to shelter us and all of our secrets,

Walls to make us feel secure and to give us a sense of peace.

When the Walls Crumble

Sometimes we may come out from behind the walls we've built

for a moment, an hour or a day,

Then we run back to our shelter until the next time we feel brave

enough to venture out.

Over time our walls begin to crumble little by little as the years

pound against them,

Some of our walls may be suddenly bulldozed by circumstances

beyond our control,

Then we're left exposed,

And something happens,

A shift and a change occur.

It's then we realize the walls that we built

were really prisons we put ourselves into,

And now that we're exposed

We're also free.

Prayer:

God, help us to see where we have put up walls that imprison us, isolate us, hold us back, and limit us, and then help us to break them down. Free us to be who you created us to be so we can walk together in love and unity as lights, visions of hope, intercessors, warriors, teachers, healers, and as your hands of love extended to a lost and hurting world. In Jesus' name we ask. Amen.

The Mind

The mind is a powerful thing,

God designed it in such a way

that it continues to evolve,

and function at levels we can't even imagine.

Its capacity to create is limitless,

Its capacity to think and imagine is amazing,

Its capacity to find solutions

and solve problems is marvelous,

Its capacity to comprehend is remarkable,

Yet its capacity to believe lies and be misled,

And to shut down to the truth,

And to form its own reality is shocking and sad.

What a waste... God must grieve...I do...

Foundation Self-Check

Our foundation is built on who we are. Who we are is based on what we believe. What we believe is based on what we put into our hearts and our minds. What we become and what we will have is based not only on what we believe but also on what we speak.

God commands us to build a firm foundation and to guard our minds, our hearts and our words. God calls us to be a light so we can encourage others and lead them to him. We must always stand united, and pray for one another so that when the storms of life engulf us, even though we might be shaken...we will not fall!

<u>Action Steps:</u>

As you read these, write down your answers. Look over your answers and reflect on what you wrote. Notice where you see a need for change or improvement. Write out ideas and steps on how you plan to make these changes.

1. Do you know who you really are? What are your core beliefs? These are what would you live and die for, what takes up your

time and money, and what you invest your life in.

2. What type of image or message do you project? Does it match who you are?

3. What kind of thoughts do you meditate on? What thoughts run through or occupy your mind?

4. Do your words encourage, build up and give life, or do they hurt, tear down, or cause death? If your words tend to be negative, figure out why and think of how you can change them.

5. Are you angry? Pray and ask God to show you if you have any unforgiveness in your heart. If so, ask God to help you forgive anyone who has hurt or wronged you, including yourself.

6. Are you connected to godly people? Do you have a good support system? Having people to pray and study the Bible with regularly is a good way to stay accountable. It will strengthen your foundation and keep you inspired.

Chapter 5

Changes

We may not like change, but we live in a world of constant

change...

I have experienced many changes in my life. I had come to a

place in life where I was very happy, content, and involved in a

lot of ministry when my world fell apart and everything changed.

I had to learn to adjust to all the changes, to trust God more, and

to believe things would get better. It was not easy. I hung on,

prayed, and pressed in, and eventually things did improve.

Not only does the world change, we continue to change

throughout our lives, hopefully for good. We should work on

growing wiser and more disciplined daily. I try to read self-help

books regularly, spend time in the Word, and I listen to lessons

on CD's, You Tube, TED talks, and the internet. Although I

spend a lot of time learning, I know I will never learn everything, but it is good to strive for more and to be prepared for what may come.

Change and growth can be both exciting and good. We must look at change in a positive light. In the light of all the good possibilities that await, the dreams that can come to pass, and the new experiences we can have. We should think of hope when we hear the word change, and hope for better things to come.

.

All Things Change

Times change,

Ideas change,

Places change,

We change,

Our likes and dislikes change.

We grow older,

Some of us grow wiser,

Some of our minds expand.

We leave some things behind,

Some we forget,

Some we reject,

Some we can't hang on to.

There is one thing that never changes,

It remains the same throughout the ages,

It is the Word of God,

It's trustworthy and true,

Powerful and mighty,

It's alive and active…

It inspires… It transforms…

It gives hope… It gives life.

Continual Change

Our lives are like the seasons,

Ever-changing,

We too plant and harvest,

And our personal seasons can go from warm to cold.

The cold seasons in our lives can cause some things to freeze and

die in us and around us.

When things begin to warm up, we find the strength to pluck and

uproot all the dead and useless things from our lives.

Then as things start to heat up our days seem to be filled with

sunshine, which can also brighten our outlook and warm our

hearts.

This causes new things to grow and sprout within and without...

Prayer:

I pray you are in a good season. If you are in a bad season, I pray you're wise enough to see what you must pluck out of your life. I pray that God gives you the ability to do what you must do. I pray for you to have the strength to believe, to hang on, to fight, to get back up when you fall, and to look forward with hope and expectation to the better season God has for you.

In Jesus' name I ask this, Amen.

A Time for Change

All things change in time,

and there is a time for change.

Things can never stay exactly the same.

Some changes are expected,

and some catch us totally off guard.

Some changes are good,

while others can be quite bad.

Some change bring us joy,

while others break our heart.

Some changes are forced on us,

Others are a welcome answer to prayer.

Positive Change

It is not because of who we are that we can change,

It is because of who He is,

And being connected to Him,

That enables us to change.

Therefore, if anyone is in Christ, he is a new creation; old things

have passed away; behold, all things have become new.

(2Corinthians 5:17 NKJV)

Power

You have power...

Power to attain wisdom,

Power to change your thoughts,

Power to change your words,

Power to change your actions,

Power to change yourself,

Power to change your future,

Power to change things around you.

You tap into your power

By seeking Christ,

By reading the Bible,

By praying,

By fasting,

By repenting,

By believing,

And by obeying.

I Change

As I read God's word I learn,

As I learn new things I grow,

As I grow I change…

As I change ...

I transform...

I change my thoughts,

I change my beliefs,

I change my actions.

I change the road I travel on,

And on this new road I change my future.

Do not remember the former things, Nor consider the things of old. Behold, I will do a new thing, Now it shall spring forth; Shall you not know it? I will even make a road in the wilderness And rivers int the desert (Isaiah 43:18-19 NKJV)

Change can be positive. I have listed some things you can change to improve your life.

Write out your answers and ideas. These will help you take a good look at your situation.

Action Steps:

1. Is your home and family life a safe place of encouragement, love, peace, and laughter? What changes can you make to improve it? Example: I will stop complaining and being negative. I can be more encouraging and supportive. I will plan fun activities like movie night, hiking, game night, and beach trips.

2. Are your friendships having a positive or negative effect on you? Your friends should be encouraging and uplifting. If they are having a negative effect on you then you should cut the time you spend with them. Strive to move forward and seek positive and motivating relationships.

3. What bad habits do you need to break? If you are not taking good care of yourself, what changes can you make that would benefit you? Example: I could work out three times a week,

walk with a friend, eat better, and look up healthy recipes. I could also go to bed at a set time in order to get 7-8 hours of sleep.

4. How about your walk with God? Could it use some adjustments? Example: I will study my bible daily and write out scriptures to encourage myself in areas where I am weak. I will join a bible study to help build a stronger foundation and give me more direction and peace.

5. How is your financial situation? Are you living paycheck to paycheck? Make a budget, track your spending, and make a payoff plan for credit card debt. Start a savings fund for repairs, trips, yearly fees, and emergencies. Think of ways to generate extra income, such as a part-time job. Find areas where you can cut expenses. Call your credit card companies and ask for a lower interest rate. I have included an example of a budget and a quick credit card payoff.

Example of a Budget and a Quick Credit Card Pay Off

House/Rent $_____   Gas $_____

Light $_____   Water/Trash $_____

Phone $_____   Food/household $_____

Car Insurance $_____   Life Insurance $_____

Gasoline $_____   Entertainment $_____

Clothing & haircuts $_____   Donations $_____

Credit cards $_____   Savings $ _____

Monthly Income $_____ - Total Monthly expenses $_____

= $_____

Now you can see what you are working with and where you
may need to make adjustments. Start two savings funds-- One for
essential expenses and the other for things you want. Being
prepared will save you from stress and give you freedom. Review
your budget regularly.

Use credit cards for emergencies. Save up cash for that outfit.
Interest on your credit card can build and cost you hundreds more
than a great sale price which had tempted you to use you card.

You have several choices on how you can pay your cards.

A) Pay the minimum and pay off in 13-20 years.

B) Pay the extra shown on your bill for a 3-year pay off.

C) Follow the simple plan below and wipe out your credit card debt in less than 3 years.

Credit	Total Owed	%	(A) Pay Min.	(B) Extra	= Payoff
Card #1	$2,070.00	26.99	$68.00	13 yr./ * $89.00	= 3 yr.
Card #2	$9,933.91	10.15	$299.99	14 yr./ $321.00	= 3 yr.
Card #3	$9,502.00	15.99	$240.00	20 yr./ $300.00	= 3 yr.

C.) The simple plan - Pay a little more, $100.00 a month on the smallest balance card #1.

When it is paid off, apply the $100.00 to card #3. You will be paying $100.00 + $240.00 Min. = $340.00 until it is paid off.

Then apply the $340.00 to card #2. You will pay $340.00 + $299.00 = $639.00 a month.

*Notice on card #1 under B that just $21.00 extra a month cuts 10 years off the loan.

Now write out all your information and work on your budget and payoff plan.

Owe no one anything except to love one another, for he who loves another has fulfilled the law. (Romans 13:8 NKJV)

Two roads diverged in a wood and I - I took the one less travelled by. And that has made all the difference

Chapter 6

Revelations

Dramatic disclosures, secrets unveiled, things brought to light....

When I spend time in God's Word, I often get thoughts, ideas, and revelations and I have to write them down quickly before I forget them. God is deep and full of wisdom; He is like a well of fresh water that never runs dry. The more we search for God and spend time with Him, the more He reveals to us.

God is able to speak to us individually through his Word. You will find there are many layers to what God will show you. You can read the same scriptures over and over again and get different messages and revelations each time. He will give us what we need and reveal what we are ready to comprehend and receive. In times when we are sick, confused, depressed, lost, lonely, betrayed, abused, or hurting, God will give us the exact words we need to hear to comfort, heal, encourage, strengthen, or instruct us. The key is to ask and search.

Prayer:

God, lead me and give me wisdom as I read your word. You know exactly what I need so I am looking at you, Father, to teach me. In Jesus' name I ask. Amen.

'Call to me and I will answer you, and show you great and mighty things, which you do not know.' (Jeremiah 33:3 NKJV)

Silence

So thick it speaks … its own language,

No words,

No songs,

No sighs,

Yet I still hear something.

It cuts,

It pierces through all that's been left unsaid,

It floats through the darkness,

It clears out the cobwebs,

It straightens out the confusion in the midst,

It aligns,

It empowers,

It directs,

Yet nothing was spoken out loud.

God Is Forever Faithful

When man tears you down,

God builds you up,

When man lies to you,

God tells you the truth,

When man hurts you,

 God comforts you,

When man robs you,

God provides.

When man crushes you,

 God restores you,

When man rejects you,

God loves you,

When man abandons you,

God is for you and with you.

My Search

In search of truth,

I found Him,

In my search for real love,

I found His heart,

In search of self,

I found it was linked with my purpose,

In search of my destiny,

I found it was tied to Him.

God Is More than Enough

When I had nothing left to physically hang onto

I realized God was all I needed.

God is more than enough

to calm my raging storms,

God is more than enough

to lead and guide me through the perils of life,

God is more than enough

to crush all my enemies,

even the ones that reside in my head.

God is more than enough

to teach me all I need to lift myself out of any pit

and rise to the mountaintops of life.

God is more than enough to give me victory and set me free.

What Does It Profit a Man to Gain the Whole World and Lose His Soul?

So what if we know everything…

But we have no real love for others.

Who will listen to us?

Who will want to be around us?

What joy is there in being a know-it-all...

if you have no one to share it with?

So what if we own the world...

But we do not own our own mind, heart and soul?

For what have we then...

If we do not even have control of ourselves?

God would ask…

Have you set a guard around your temple?

Who has your ear, your heart, and your mind?

What have you done with your soul?

Life is Full of Choices

Life becomes about the choices we make,

Our choices will determine what we will have,

And our choices will help define who we become.

While our choices help make us who we are,

The mind is the controlling factor,

Because what we believe in our minds

Will set the limits we place on ourselves,

This will influence the choices we make.

We do what we believe we can,

We become what we think we are,

Our mind will either enable us or hinder us,

It will give us the ability to take chances,

To grow and discover new paths and opportunities,

Or it will keep us in a holding pattern

Locked behind the doors of the past.

The Bible tells us that *"as a man thinketh in his heart, so is he"*
(Proverbs 23:7 KJV)

What is Sad?

Sad is growing old

and never having really lived,

Sad is believing the enemy's lies

and not God's truths,

Sad is letting love pass you by

because your heart was filled with fear,

Sad is holding onto anger and hate

and not allowing forgiveness to free you from your prison.

Sad is forgetting how to smile after a good cry,

Sad is falling down and refusing to fight your way back up,

Sad is growing old alone because you wanted everyone to be

perfect even though perfection is impossible,

Sad is always wanting everything your own way

like a spoiled child,

Sad is looking so hard for blessings

that you forget to be a blessing to others.

Choices

The beginning or the end,

Good or bad,

Happy or sad,

Truth or lies,

Remembering or forgetting,

Love or hate,

Passion or passive,

Stale or fresh,

Observe or participate,

Forgiveness or anger.

There are always choices to be made...

We pick our

Attitudes,

Words,

Roads,

and our actions.

The Word warns us to consider the cost of our choices.

There are consequences,

And prices that must be paid.

Regrets

The things we never do,

The places we never visit,

The people we never see,

The things we never say,

The secrets we keep in our hearts,

The love we hide or deny,

The anger we refuse to let go of,

The forgiveness we do not give,

These are some of the things

that may become regrets

in the end...

Questions to Ponder

I believe many of us have regrets about some of the choices we have made in our lives. We usually have several options when selecting our careers, schools, jobs, friends, where we live, and who we marry. It is only logical to wonder, especially if the choices we made did not turn out as we expected, what our lives would be like if we had chosen differently.

I have questioned some of my decisions when they did not turn out good. I had numerous opportunities and at times it was hard to decide. Sometimes I did not feel prepared enough, I lacked confidence, or I was fearful. I have wondered about the career path I took, the jobs and promotions I did not take, the colleges, the vacations and other offers I passed up, and the men I did not marry.

In my college days, I had a chance to live in Germany with my uncle and his family while he was stationed there, but fear of the unknown held me back. I feel like I may have let some great opportunities get away and I have tried to imagine not just what my life would be like, but what I might be like had I selected different paths. Have you ever wondered "What if?" and felt like you lost out on a great opportunity, relationship, or an exciting adventure and regretted a choice you made?

Are there some doors you wish you had avoided or things you could go back and change? There are some doors I wish I had never entered. If I knew then what I know now, I could have seen the red flags and run the other way. I could have saved so much time, heartache, and pain.

There are secrets we guard and secrets we spill. Sometimes we say too much or too little. Perhaps you shared something told to you in private and the results were not good. Maybe you kept silent about the way you felt about someone you loved out of fear of rejection and found out later that they cared for you and were waiting for you to make a move or give them a sign.

Many times, we made the choices we made due to limited knowledge and resources. We may have said and done things out of anger, foolishness, immaturity or lack of self-control. That was probably the best we could do at the time. Whatever was the case, there is really no point in dwelling on all the things we should have done. What we can do is deal with what we have, work on improving the things we are able to, release our regrets, and forgive ourselves so we can have inner peace.

Prayer:

God, forgive me and help me to forgive myself for any wrong choices I have made in my life and for all the things I never should have said or done. God, help me let go of all my regrets and make the best of my current situation. Give me wisdom, boldness, and strength to make wiser choices and to take the correct road, even if it means walking alone.

Help me grow in your ways and in the fruit of the spirit so I have the discipline to speak when and how I should, and to keep silent when it is better that I say nothing. Fill me with childlike belief and anticipation to expect good things and to attain them. Strengthen me for my journey and help me always to pick the path that is best for me. In Jesus' name I ask. Amen.

Chapter 7

New Seasons

Endings can be sad, but with each ending there can be the start of something new...

I was born in the summer. When I was younger, this was always my favorite time of the year. I called myself a summer baby. They are many things I enjoyed in the summer--like ice cream, shorts, bare feet, riding bikes, swimming, skating, making mud pies, playing in our tree house, the long hot days, and the cool nights, and staying up late playing games with family and friends. I still love doing some of these things and I have added a few more. Watching the waves crashing on the beach, taking photos of beautiful beach sunsets, my bare feet on the cool wet sand, summer fruits, outdoor concerts, walking with my childhood friend Margaret in the evening before dusk, and the sounds of my neighbor's water fountain by my open bedroom window.

When I was young, summers seemed to go on almost forever, which made me happy because it gave me so much time to play. Now by the end of August, I find myself looking forward to the end of summer and longing for cooler weather and other things the new season brings.

Winter, spring, summer, and fall, every season serves a purpose and holds its own beauty and wonder. We need the rain, snow, and the dying and falling off of flowers and leaves. Just as we need new growth, flourishing flowers, and vegetation. Our lives, like the seasons, endure pruning of some of our ways or things we need to release, cold times of isolation, the death of ideas and dreams. We also have times of transformation, new situations, and new life. The spring season with all the blossoming beautiful colors and shapes filling the landscape speaks to me of God's promises, and it gives hope of change, new beginnings, and better things to come.

Ecclesiastes tells us there is a season and a time for every purpose. Life is so much easier when we are aware of what season we are in, and we learn not just how to survive but also how to flow in our current season while hanging onto the promise of a better season.

To everything there is a season, A time for every purpose under heaven:

A time to be born, And a time to die;

A time to plant, And a time to pluck what is planted;

A time to kill, And a time to heal;

A time to break down, And a time to build up;

A time to weep, And a time to laugh;

A time to mourn, And a time to dance;

A time to cast away stones, And a time to gather stones;

A time to embrace, And a time to refrain from embracing;

A time to gain, And a time to lose;

A time to keep, And a time to throw away;

A time to tear, And a time to sew;

A time to keep silence, And a time to speak;

A time to love, And a time to hate;

A time of war, And a time of peace.

(Ecclesiastes 3-8 NKJV)

It's a New Season

A season of healing

and learning,

A season of growing

and moving forward,

 A season of gaining vision

and planning,

 A season of setting boundaries

within and without,

Until at last the revival in my soul can sing a new song

And push me forward with its fire once again...

Summer is Here

In all its splendor,

Its long hot days and its refreshing nights,

Day trips and vacations,

Outdoor concerts and plays,

Games, picnics and parties,

Barbecues and watermelon,

Swimming, umbrellas, and pools,

Sand and bare feet,

Waves and sunsets on the beach,

Long walks and long talks...

Camping, tents, campfires, and marshmallows,

Light-hearted moods, songs, laughter, and merriment.

Memories of childhood dance in my head

refreshing me and filling me with energy and curiosity

to check out this new day and how I can play,

Oh, the beauty of a summer day!

Seasons of Transformation

Like the seasons, we go through long cold, winters of the soul,

where we have loss and we have to say goodbye to situations,

places, jobs, or people,

We may move, things may go cold or end, and our way of life

changes,

At times we're numbed by the severity of the pain.

Then spring comes with all its hope and promise, and it beckons

us to get up and move on,

 New things sprout up and encourage us to believe for more,

Then summer is upon us and it warms the land and our soul,

 Excitement fills the air,

The sun shines on a landscape of beautiful colors, shapes, and

smells,

Everything seems possible as new adventures, people, and

opportunities call out to us,

And life flourishes and goes on.

Maybe you have had a long, hard winter that just seemed to drag on.

Let the summer in your soul inspire you to rise and move past the hard times,

Look around, see and reach for new treasures, experiences, and friendships.

God will always give us another chance, and another start,

I pray you trust God and move forward, and as you take that first step

may he empower you to search for more opportunities,

And may you also make some of your own.

I pray that with God's help you're able to create the best summer of your life!

A New Day

So many things become clear

in the light of a new day.

Sometimes we need rain to wash away

all the former pain.

A new sun can bring so much hope,

And a blue sky

can infuse joy...

If you look forward,

If you refuse to look back,

If you learn from your mistakes

and determine to do better

and have better,

Then anything is possible

with a new day!

The Butterfly...

Lives a life of transformation...

It starts out not so lovely,

Then it goes through a time of transition

where it is secluded in a cocoon.

Something wonderful happens.

It is infused with beauty,

And when it emerges from the cocoon,

It breaks free with the glorious change.

Its colors are breathtaking,

And it is given the gift of flight.

It can now reach new heights that it could never reach before...

We are like the butterfly in many ways...

It is not until God gets us alone and does a transformation on us

that our lives become a thing of beauty...

And do not be conformed to this world, but be transformed by the renewing of your mind, that you may prove what is that good and acceptable and perfect will of God. (Romans 12:2 NKJV)

Where Does Time Go?

We rush here and there,

We do this and that,

We get caught up in doing so many things

we can lose our way,

and wear ourselves out.

Now is a good time to step back,

Reflect and see where you're at.

Are you making good use of your time?

Are you taking care of the important things?

Or are you just spinning your wheels

and going in circles?

What have you accomplished?

What have you missed

or not attended to as you should have?

The Value of Time...

Time flies by,

It escapes us,

Our days are full,

Our tasks are many,

And time runs out...

It really waits for no man.

Time is Limited – Use it Wisely

Action Steps

1. Are you doing things to improve yourself and your life? Write out a time-line of what you have accomplished in your life. Compare your past to your present. Have you seen improvements in the use of your time and resources?

2. Now is a good time to mention goals. How are you doing with your goals? If you do not have goals, pray and ask God to help you write out some goals for your life for 1-year, 3-year, 5-year, etc. God said, "My people perish for lack of knowledge." It is a fact that successful people plan and set goals, and then they do the work and research to attain them. These are life goals, like schooling, a new job skill, becoming a leader or speaker, starting a company, etc. Once you set your goals, break them down into quarterly, monthly and daily tasks. Your goals should be in at least two places: On a sheet of paper to keep in front of you, and one in your planner to work on daily. Give

yourself small rewards when you stay on task, at least once weekly and a bigger one monthly.

3. We all need to dream and have fun things to look forward to. Are there things you want to experience? Write out a bucket list of fun things you want to learn, places you would like to visit, and things you want to do. Write them all down, no matter how big or small.

4. Pray for creative ways to acquire the funds for your goals and your bucket list.

5. Are you spending enough time with people who matter to you? Figure out what you can do to create some fun, memorable times to show them that they are special to you.

6. The big question. Does God get the best part of your time or are you giving God scraps?

   Where can you make more time for God in prayer, Bible-reading, and listening? Put it in your planner and set your alarm under God time. This way it will become a priority.

Chapter 8

Truths

A little white lie or a big fat lie are the same, A lie is a lie is a

lie....

Tell me the truth and set me free...

There is nothing like the truth. Nothing is as good as the truth. It can be simple yet profound. Truth, reality, actuality, correctness, rightness, validity, factualness. Sometimes hard to swallow, but it is the fact. Truth is the truth--nothing should be added or taken away. There is no need to embellish it, disguise it, or hide it. Yet we do.

Some people cannot tell the truth, some people cannot accept the truth so they hide from it, and some cannot handle the truth. The truth cannot be hidden; it will expose itself in time. It can take years or decades, but I know it happens. I have seen it happen many times.

The truth has the ability to do so many things. While lies can keep us bound and in the dark, it is the truth that can set us free. This is why I seek the truth. I prefer to face the facts, even if they are not pretty, than to continue to live with lies. In the end it is the lies that can hurt us the most. They can blindside us, crush us, and destroy us.

Then Jesus said to those Jews who believed Him, "If you abide in my word, you are my disciples indeed. And you shall know the truth, and the truth shall make you free." (John 8:31-32 NKJV) Let not mercy and truth forsake you; Bind them around your neck, Write them on the tablet of your heart, And so find favor and high esteem In the sight of God and man. (Proverbs 3:3-4 NKJV)

My Shattering Truth

My truth hit me like a ton of bricks,

I had danced around it for a while,

I skirted this way and that,

I dreamed about it,

I peeked at its sharp edges,

I even cut myself a time or two,

Somehow, I knew.

Isn't that always the case?

It was too terrifying to fully face,

Life altering,

Devasting.

It took my breath away for more than a moment,

It knocked me off balance,

Then it floored me,

And when I tried to run from it,

 It chased me down,

Until it ran me over like a bulldozer.

What Now?

We look,

We hunger,

We search,

We wonder...

Then we ask...

What now, Lord?

God has watched us,

He has waited for us...

To get to this point

Of desperation,

Of want.

No more game playing,

God wants us to get serious

And get down to business!

When we ask, what now, God?

He will answer us and show us the way.

Because I Asked...

I asked for more faith,

And I was stretched,

I asked for greater love,

And my heart was broken.

I asked for more wisdom,

And I had to go through many obstacles.

I asked for comfort,

And many were sent to me so that I could comfort them.

I asked for a teacher,

And I was moved to teach the needy.

I asked for a leader,

And now I have many who insist on following me.

God has an unusual way of giving us what we ask for...

Yet through it all,

I have been blessed

far more than I could have imagined.

Why?

Why do we run

when we should walk?

Why do we talk

when we should listen?

Why do we give up

when we should stand and believe?

Why do we leave

when we should stay?

Why do we hate those we should love,

And love those we should hate?

Believe...

Believe that nothing is too big for God,

Believe that nothing is impossible for God,

Believe in God and get in line with His will,

And you shall have the desires of your heart.

Trust in the Lord, and do good; Dwell in the land, and feed on

His faithfulness. Delight yourself also in the Lord, And He shall

give you the desires of your heart. (Psalm 37:3-4 NKJV)

Thanksgiving...

Thankful for life,

For living,

For the air we breathe and the nourishment we take in.

Thankful for good health,

For our families and loved ones,

For connections and favor.

Thankful for the sun and light and the beautiful sky,

For all the beauty of plants and flowers,

For the changes in the season,

For the rain and snow.

Thankful for all that God provides,

For His love, mercy, wisdom, knowledge, peace and joy!

Yes, we are to be thankful for all He gives so freely...

Life Happens

Life Happens as we're busy running back and forth,

Even when something tragic happens... life goes on.

No one gets to pick where they are born, or their parents or

siblings,

No one gets a perfect life handed to them,

No matter what you get... life goes on.

You do get to choose how you react to things,

Your attitude and your values,

Your likes and dislikes, what you will accept or reject,

What road you take when you grow up... if you grow up,

Some of us never do... But life still goes on.

Whether we choose to be happy or sad,

If the choices we make are good or bad,

Whether we are filled with love or hate,

Whether we choose to give or take,

If we use people or help people…life still goes on.

We choose who we will serve, and how we will serve,

We choose the quality of our life when we choose to follow God

or reject him...

And life still goes on…

No Turning Back

There is no going left or right,

There is no turning back.

The road is high,

The road is low,

The road is narrow,

The road can be lonely,

But there is only one way for me,

There is no giving up,

There is no turning back.

I have decided,

I have made my choice,

I have picked my side,

And chosen my path,

There is no turning back.

The Simple Things

The simple things are what really matter,

A smile,

A hug,

Loyalty,

Morals,

Time,

Laughter,

Family,

Friends,

Bonding,

Salvation and God.

It is the simple things that are more costly than gold,

It is the simple things that bring true joy and peace to your soul,

It's these things that you really need in your life,

and that money cannot buy...

Salvation and the Holy Spirit are like precious treasure ,

Yet they are easy to attain...for they are free gifts from God.

Getting to God's Will

What is it you seek?

What is it you need to know?

What is it you long for?

What is your heart's desire?

God would ask...

Are you in my will?

Learn to listen to my spirit in you.

I give you peace like no other.

Align yourself with me and my ways...

and there I am.

I am the still small voice,

The feeling of peace within you…

As you search for me and my ways...

Here I am... feel me,

Here I am... see me,

Here I am… reach out to me.

Where is Joy Found?

Sometimes you must look forward,

And refuse to look back,

You must not allow fear to keep you down

or hold you captive.

If you're afraid to move on,

and you continue to live

in a past of anger and regrets,

you can't really live.

You have already buried yourself…

in a coffin of limitations,

and in the ground of fear.

There is joy in new beginnings

and in new opportunities.

There is excitement and wonder in fresh starts.

Joy is simple yet profound.

It's a gift from God,

It is birthed in your attitude,

brought about by appreciation...

of the exceptional and the ordinary.

There is joy in the smell of fresh coffee in the morning,

In the song of a bird outside your window,

In a fresh breeze on a hot day,

In the laughter of family as you gather.

There is joy in meeting new people,

And in exploring different adventures...

Oh, the possibilities are endless...

Don't limit yourself...

and don't limit what God can do.

Don't lie down and give up,

Rattle those dry bones,

Rise up and live,

And expect good things to happen,

We have an amazing Father!

... Do not sorrow, for the joy of the Lord is your strength."
(Nehemiah 8:10 NKJV)

In Memory of Dad

I thought of you today and I cried...

I thought of all the things you said,

and the things you will never say…

And I shed a silent tear.

I thought of all the things you did,

and all the things you will never do…

And I shed a silent tear.

I thought of all the people you impacted with your love,

and all the people who will never get to know you…

And I shed a silent tear.

I thought of your joy and kindness,

And the silly things you did to make us laugh…

And I shed a silent tear.

I cried on the inside, yet I smile on the outside

as I reflect on how blessed we were to have you as a father,

I wonder if you ever look down and see us.

If you do, I pray we make you proud.

You loved deeply,

And you taught us so much by example.

You instilled so many things in us…

Your love, kindness, compassion, strength,

wisdom, humor, and joy shone like a bright light

in this dark world.

We have tried to follow your examples,

And we have passed them on to our children and friends.

And so you live on...

In our minds and hearts,

And in our actions.

Chapter 9

This Crazy Faith Which Hopes Against All Odds

Faith that moves mountains…

As we were talking one day, my daughter Allison said, "Mom we're addicted to hope because we believe in God so much and we've seen what He can do. We know He can do anything. So, it's hard to let go of some things when we know He can turn any situation around."

I said, "You're right, Allison, we're not putting our hope in man, who is not always faithful, but in God who can do miracles. It's hard for some people to understand or to fully comprehend why we do what we do. We've seen too much. That's why we have this crazy faith."

We all need hope. It is what gives us reason to go on. What do we have if we do not have hope to dream or hope to hang on? You can go through many things and suffer loss and bounce back if you have hope in God that things will get better. Hope is a wish, a feeling of expectation and desire for a certain thing to happen. Faith is a belief, a confidence, a reliance and dependence, or complete trust, in somebody or something but without logical proof. Hope is tied to faith. It is an anchor for the mind, heart, and soul. In this fallen world we sometimes desperately need hope and faith to survive. Tie your hope to faith in the one true God.

This hope we have as an anchor of the soul, both sure and steadfast, and which enters the Presence behind the veil, (Hebrews6:9 NKJV)

So then faith cometh from hearing, and hearing by the word of God. (Romans 10:17 NKJV)

Crazy Faith and Hope

God, you calm the storms

in my life and in my heart,

You have healed me and my children numerous times,

You saved all us all from the many hands of death,

You opened doors that seemed impossible to open,

You moved in mighty ways,

You even parted my Red Sea.

You are...

The God of Miracles,

The God of power,

The God of love,

The God of mercy,

The God of this crazy faith and hope within my soul!

Trust in the Lord and do good; Dwell in the land, and feed on

His faithfulness. Delight yourself also in the Lord, And he shall give you the desires of you heart. Commit your way to the Lord,

Trust also in Him, And He shall bring it to pass. He shall bring

forth your righteousness as the light, And your justice as the

noonday. (Psalm 37:3-6 NKJV)

I am a Prisoner of Hope

because I know the One I believe in

will always come through for me.

Why?

 In times when everything was against me

God has always been with me,

God has always restored me.

And when I pray for my hurting or lost friends,

I have seen God's hand move in their lives in incredible ways.

Your mercy, O Lord, is in the heavens; Your faithfulness reaches

to the clouds. (Psalm 36:5 NKJV)

What is Hope?

Hope is a desire,

A wish,

A thing you want to see come to pass.

We all go through trials because we all live in a fallen world,

Our child may be a prodigal son... and we hope he comes home,

We may have a financial loss... and hope we can recover,

We may have a break-up... and hope the relationship can be restored,

We might even lose everything we own... and hope we can get back up.

I love the passage in Zechariah 9:12, where God tells us to return to the stronghold... the place that He has fortified to protect us from attack,

And He calls us you "prisoners of hope."

And then He promises that even today He will restore double to us.

What an awesome promise He has given us! He is telling us to put our hope in Him and to return to His stronghold. He will answer if we follow what He tells us to do,

Prayer:

I am that prisoner of hope. God, help me return to your stronghold and forgive me for my sins and for moving out. Restore all that has been lost or taken from me. Help me to stay close to you all the days of my life. In Jesus' name I ask.

Crazy Hope

When all seems lost

And you see no hint of a breakthrough,

When it seems that every door is shut,

Nothing is working out,

and everyone has given up.

Yet something deep within you cries out,

Telling you not to give up,

It tells you to hope and believe that it can happen,

To pray and look to God for a miracle.

So, against all odds,

Despite every negative thought coming at you,

Against every stronghold and obstacle,

You take a stand.

It is you and God,

against all the circumstances.

Something deep inside you rises up,

You dare to see it, to believe it,

And then you declare it.

You wait,

And with that crazy hope,

You expect.

Faith to Believe

It takes faith…

to get up in the morning

and to keep pressing forward when everything is against you.

It takes faith…

to believe that what seems impossible

will come to pass.

It takes faith…

to keep on believing

when everyone else has given up.

It takes faith…

to look upon utter chaos

and be at peace that it will all work out.

It takes faith…

to face your giant with the confidence that you will fight and win.

It takes great faith…

to believe in a great God you cannot see,

but this is what God says He requires.

"Therefore know that the Lord your God, He is God, the faithful God who keeps covenant and mercy for a thousand generations with those who love Him and keep his commandments;

(Deuteronomy 7:9 NKJV)

My Maker and My Hope, I Know Who He is, Do You?

My heart sings,

My feet dance,

My mind is filled with wonder,

My face is full of delight,

And I am filled with hope,

Because I know my maker.

He is my teacher,

My savior,

My leader,

My protector,

My king,

My shelter,

My mountain mover,

My comforter,

My hero,

My rock,

My lion,

My fortress,

My warrior,

My light,

My father,

and my friend.

Faith

Faith is believing in the unseen.

It is knowing,

It is trusting,

It is expecting,

It is waiting,

It is seeing it in your mind's eye,

As if it has already taken place.

Prayer:

God, give me the strength to anchor my mind, heart, and soul to you and to your word. God,

I ask that you would grant me the ability to have complete unwavering hope and faith in you, no matter what comes at me. Help my faith not waiver even an inch so that I can accomplish whatever you put before me to do. In Jesus' name I ask. Amen.

Dream

There should be a dream within each of us.

It is what gives us a reason to rise each day,

And to get back up after each fall.

The dream puts the fight in us and the fire under us,

And the hope within our eyes.

The dream gives us desire ...

It calls out to us,

To reach and to strive,

To imagine and to do,

To believe ... and to become,

It gives us a reason to live.

I can do all things through Christ who strengthens me.

(Philippians 4:13 NKJV)

May Your Heart Sing

May your every thought be covered with God's peace,

May you see the beauty in all things made by God's hand,

May your life bring you joy and excitement,

May you find pleasure in the simple things,

May the sun always shine through for you,

May you have gentle breezes to keep you cool,

And sunsets to paint you a beautiful sky,

May each new day touch you in a special way

Until it makes your heart sing...

I waited patiently for the Lord; and He inclined to me, And heard my cry. He also brought me up out of a horrible pit, Out of the miry clay, And set my feet upon a rock, And established my steps. He has put a new song in my mouth – Praise to our God; Many will see it and fear, And will trust in the Lord. (Psalm 40:1-3 NKJV)

Chapter 10

Life is Fragile – Handle with Love

Love so powerful, it changed the world...

Opportunities come and go, doors open and close, people come into our lives and leave. Life is fragile and short. Not only is life fragile, so are people. With all that goes on in the world, people are in need of love. My spiritual mother use to tell our prayer group not to pray or minister to anyone if we do not have love. She was right. We cannot help anyone if we do not love them. I have seen people behave in ways that were rude, judging, harsh and very hurtful, and the results were not good. I have also witnessed when people minister in love. It is true there is something special that happens when you have God's love in your heart and you pray and minister to someone who is broken and hurting. They can feel love's power, and they are able to be healed, delivered, filled with hope, and empowered by God as He breathes new life into them.

Many people come into our lives for a short time. Things happen, new situations occur, people move on, some pass on, and they leave us with only memories. Some people are like dreams which slip in and out of our lives too quickly. We should love and encourage those we know and those whose paths cross ours for a season or a minute. It takes only a few seconds to give someone a kind word or a smile; they are both free, yet they carry the power to lift a hurting soul or a lonely heart.

The International Picture of the Year about wearing blue on Fridays in support of our troops moved me, brought tears to my eyes, and inspired me to write this chapter. I hope that these writings speak to you and that they stir your soul to love more, to be more, and to do more.

Outrageous Love

The spirit is saying outrageous love is our weapon,

Outrageous love is our armor,

Outrageous love is our hope,

Outrageous love is our core,

Outrageous love binds us to our maker,

Outrageous love leads us,

Outrageous love guides us,

And becomes our compass,

As we allow it to fill us and flow through us.

Prayer:

God, may your outrageous love always fill our hearts to
overflowing so we can be your vessels to love others. May we not
care what some people may think of us as we move in your ways.
May we have no fear in loving, in being, or in doing as you
would lead us.

In Jesus' name we ask you, God, let it be so. Amen.

Let all that you do be done with love. (1Corinthians 16:14 NKJV)

Love...

The greatest need

is also the very thing God told us to do,

Yet we do not listen as we should.

We all need to feel loved...and wanted.

We all need to feel we belong.

Man with all his witty inventions...

Has only put more distance between us.

We get busy... and so distracted...

That many of us cannot even hear our loved ones

crying out for attention.

We all long for attention and love,

We need to come out from behind all the walls

and prisons and limitations we have placed before ourselves,

We need to look about,

We need to listen,

And we need to reach out in love,

before it is too late...

and we have to pay the price of all our distractions.

Who is crying out for your love today?

Prayer:

God, open our blind eyes so we can see those who are hurting

and in need. Direct our path and strengthen our walk. Fill us

with your wisdom so we know what to say. Fill us with your

boldness and power to do what needs to be done. Teach us to

truly love as you love, with no limitations, so that we can show

our love to those who need to see and feel it right now. God, help

your hurting people and allow us to be your vessels. In Jesus'

name I ask you, God, let it be so. Amen.

For God so loved the world that He gave His only begotten Son,

that whoever believes in Him should not perish but have

everlasting life. For God did not send His Son into the world to condemn the world, but that the world through Him might be

saved. (John 3:16-17 NKJV)

.

Why not Love?

Why not give,

instead of taking?

Why not believe,

instead of doubting?

Why not build up,

instead of tearing down?

Why not be soft,

instead of being hard?

Why not appreciate,

instead of taking for granted?

Why not love,

instead of hating?

You shall not take vengeance, nor bear any grudge against the children of your people, but you shall love your neighbor as yourself: I am the Lord. (Leviticus 19:18 NKJV)

This Fragile Life

The time we have is limited,

Our days are numbered,

And life is short.

Why do many of us not make the most out of every day?

Why do we let fear control and limit us or hold us back from

what we really want?

Why don't we humble ourselves and be more real

and not care so much about how we look or sound?

Why don't we have more fun and spread more joy around?

Why do we not love with all our hearts even if we get hurt?

Why do we not speak encouraging words that build up and

empower everyone we encounter?

Who knows how much time we have left to say and show

our love to our family and friends?

Why not start today?

Think of different ways to say I love you, start with words and

then move to action,

Give, expecting nothing in return.

You will be blessed back, you'll be filled with joy,

 Because you didn't expect or demand anything.

May you be blessed in mighty ways,

Because you choose to live His way.

Chapter 11

Prayer

What is Prayer?

Prayer is simple,

Yet profound,

Ordinary,

Yet extraordinary.

Prayer moves the hand of God

And the hand of God

Moves the nations.

Prayer touches the places

That nothing else can reach,

In ways that you cannot even imagine...

Pray and you change

Not only yourself

But your world.

Prayer

There is power in prayer when you're connected to

the almighty one…

While attending various Bible studies, I was asked what my

thoughts were on prayer. I was asked to write an article on prayer

in Prayer magazine, and while teaching Bible studies the

questions about prayer come up often. The topic of prayer is very

interesting. I know I am not the only person who is curious about

how other people pray. I was also curious on how prayers were

answered. From what kind of answers they got, how long it took

to get an answer, to how people waited. I use to wonder if certain

prayers had more power or the people praying them had more

power. I am the type to ask a lot of questions and take notes. I

have found that there are many factors that come into play, from

our walk with God, the way we pray, our capacity to believe, our

ability to receive what we are asking for, and if the thing we are

asking for is right for us. We can also do things that hinder our

prayers or cancel them. God in his infinite wisdom knows what we need and what is best for us, so He may answer our prayer with a long wait or a no.

I have come to see prayer in a whole new light. Prayer was a private thing for me. When I was in my early 30s, I was asked to pray out loud in a group. Never having prayed out loud and being a little shy, I passed on the offer. I also felt inadequate as my prayers were too simple in comparison to some people I had heard pray. I had tried practicing the way I had heard a few other people pray, but it was not me. One day during home Bible studies, our pastor put us into smaller groups and told us to pray for the person on the left of us. Of course, he was on my left. The pastor stepped away for a moment and I remember my ex-husband laughing as he asked me if I was going to tell the pastor, "I do not pray out loud." When he returned although I was nervous, I prayed for him. It happened again at a Women's Retreat I was leading. When I had us break for prayer, several women circled around me and asked me to pray for them. Again, I felt I was put in a position where it would be rude or hurtful to refuse to pray, so I asked God for help and prayed for them. I have found that God does have His ways of stretching us. Later some of the women ran into my ex-husband and told him how I had prayed for them at the Women's Retreat and how they were touched. They said that I had a beautiful way of praying. I think God wanted me to be encouraged because my prayers were very simple prayers.

Their remarks motivated me to pray out loud for more people, because I saw the blessings in prayer. I found that when you pray out loud for someone, they are encouraged, they know you care as they listen to your prayer and when God answers they know it came from God. As I prayed for more people, God continued to encourage me. Over the years I joined prayer groups and I started prayer groups and I have been blessed to see God answer many of the prayers in interesting ways.

Prayers do not have to be long or have fancy wording. They should not be repetitive or complaining. You do not have to be loud or yell, because God is not deaf. God knows what we or the person we are praying for is going through, so we do not have to air dirty laundry. Prayers can be simple; they just need to be real and heartfelt. The Our Father prayer is a good outline. Honor him, thank him, repent, forgive others, and ask for what you want or need.

I have grown a lot in my prayer life. I pray for everything all the time, from the small to the huge. I pray out loud or in my head depending on the situation. I pray for a parking space when I really need one, I ask God to help me unplug my sink when I cannot afford a plumber, I ask him to protect me as I drive. I pray for strength, wisdom, and direction. I pray for friends, family and leaders. I pray for the impossible, I pray for miracles and I continually see His hand move.

I also pray for God to gently correct me when I am wrong and to forgive me. I pray for God to help me change the things I know are wrong with me, the things I am unaware of, and the things that are not pleasing to Him.

I like that song, "I am a friend of God." I recently read something about being God's friend. Like Abraham, we can ask God to change His mind and have mercy on us and on our loved ones. I have seen way too much not to believe in God or in who

God is. I have seen His mighty hand move in amazing ways and I have witnessed many miracles in my family and with my friends and acquaintances.

I was looking over some of my old writings and found something on how we do not see how God is moving and working on our problems or our prayers for others. Just because we do not see anything does not mean that He is not working on it, or on a person. Change takes a long time. Many of us are quite set in our ways, even fearing change and things we cannot quite understand. Sometimes we resist the things or changes God is trying to do in our lives. Our resistance to change can delay our prayers being answered. Another problem is that we may not like the answers God give us. Because He is all- knowing he may tell us no, wait, or to do something we do not want to do. He may even give us something different than what we thought we needed or wanted.

Because Satan constantly lies to us, tries to wear us out, and trick us, we must pray without ceasing. We must stay close to God in His word and in our prayer time so that we know without a doubt who God is. We also have to know that if we are His, He hears and answers every prayer. God has said that our prayers need our belief for Him to answer. If we cannot believe, then we should not waste our breath praying. God cannot work with unbelief. Believing comes by hearing the word of God. So, wherever our belief is weak, we must search out scriptures and write them out. Then we must read them out loud daily so that we can build up our faith.

I heard a story a long time ago about how God had His angels working on something and then He suddenly told them to stop. They asked why he stopped them. God told them that the person started to doubt and he cannot work in unbelief. Wow! That really spoke to me. What a vivid picture! Although I believe, how many times have I questioned or doubted God? Because even though I believe God can do anything, sometimes the situation seems so impossible or hopeless or people are so stubborn. So, when I have concerns or doubts, I now say "God, I believe, but help my unbelief." The moral of this story is that we have to guard our words. There can be no doubts in our mind or in our heart and no negative words in our mouths. They are like poison that can hurt us, our situation, and others.

Think of this.... God spoke and He created the world. He gave us His power so that when we speak, we create our world. I have told my children this. We create our world by how we speak and treat those around us. We can speak kind, loving, encouraging words, and be patient with people. Or we can tear people down, curse them and be rude and hateful. You get back what you give out. What do you want in your world? I choose to have love, encouragement, faith, and hope. Remember, your words have power; guard them.

So then faith cometh by hearing, and hearing by the word of God
(Romans 10:17 NKJV)
Rejoice always, pray without ceasing, in everything give thanks;
for this is the will of God in Christ Jesus for you.
(1Thessalonians 5:16-18 NKJV)

Prayer is the Key

Prayer is the answer to the questions you ask,

For warfare and victory the answer is prayer,

For wisdom and knowledge prayer is the key,

God heals and restores us through prayer,

God sends his angels to assist us when we pray to God to send

them,

Prayer comforts and soothes the soul,

Prayer can answer every need,

To get closer to God, it is prayer that ushers the way in,

Prayer helps people find salvation,

Prayer strengthens the mind, body, and soul,

Everything is tied into our prayers,

Prayer moves the hand of God,

And God then rocks the world.

Then He spoke a parable to them, that men always ought to pray

and not lose heart, *(Luke 18:1 NKJV)*

The Lord is near to all who call upon Him, To all who call upon Him in truth. He will fulfill the desire of those who fear Him; He also will hear their cry and save them. The Lord preserves all who love Him, But all the wicked He will destroy. (Psalm 145:18-20 NKJV)

My Prayer and Blessing for You...

That Life would not catch you off guard,

That you would always be ready

for whatever comes at you.

That you would know when and how

to fight and win,

That you would set healthy boundaries,

That you would protect your heart,

your mind and your body,

That you would remember how to love

with your whole heart,

holding nothing back.

That the world would never change you...

That only God would transform you.

That you would always let the little child within you

come out to play,

to believe,

to dream,

and to create miracles for you.

Thoughts for your personal life...

<u>Action Steps:</u>

While we cannot control the world, we do have control of our actions. We decide how we interact with others. Think about this for a minute. The number one place we have influence on is in our home. It is our little piece of the world that we have the power to create the way we want for ourselves and others. Our homes should be a safe place filled with love, fellowship, laughter, understanding, mercy, and forgiveness. A place where we can relax, heal, have some fun, and refresh ourselves and our family and friends.

Spend some time in prayer and ask God to help you make your home your ideal place. We all need to have a special place. It is good to have some comfortable areas to sit in with nice relaxing things like beautiful pictures, some plants, and good music to soothe the soul. We get busy living and can easily forget to pay attention to the most important places, people, and details in our lives. You can start small. Think about what type of world you want to create and write at least three things that you will

start to do this week to create it.

I want my world to look and feel like

_____

_____

I will

_____

_____

I will

_____

_____

I will

_____

_____

I will

_____

_____

I will

_____

_____

I will

_____

_____

I will

_____

_____

I will

_____

_____

I will

_____

_____

Plans and Goals

<u>Action Steps</u>

The majority of people never set regular goals, so I think they need to be mentioned again. Where have you succeeded, where have you failed and what do you still want to accomplish? Some examples: Save for retirement, buy a home, get a better job, get a degree, lose 30 pounds, learn some new skills, make some new friends. Here are some steps to reach your goals.

1. Get a journal or just a plain piece of paper and write down your goals. This will remind you and encourage you to work towards accomplishing them.

2. Make an outline out of your list and set some time frames. Example below:

    In six months, I will

    _____

    In one year, I will

    _____

3. To stay on track, break your goal down into a quarterly time frame so you can review your progress every 90 days. Write boldly in your planner in the monthly calendar section "90 Day Goal Day #1." Number your goal days in red. In 30 days, write in bold "Day #30". Do the same for the 60- and 90-day mark. Repeat until you reach goals.

4. Break the things you need to do into smaller chunks and write them in the monthly sections. Then divide them and put them into your weekly sections within that month. Example: Make calls to banks, work on project with Andrew, do more research, etc.

5. A good way to help flesh out all your ideas is to do a mind map. Write out your goal on the center of a sheet of paper, then circle it. Next, draw lines coming out of the circle and write down any ideas that come to mind that will help you achieve your goal. You can also brainstorm with a friend.

Chapter 12

Thoughts are powerful; they can transform your life...

Thoughts for the Week - Weekly Challenges

Take a weekly challenge. As you read each thought for the week,

let it sink into your mind. Write down any ideas you get on how

you can apply them to your life for the week. You may find that

you like the way they impact your life and you may continue

doing them.

1. Thought for the Week... Expect

Live each day expecting good things. This means being

filled with anticipation. What does that look like? It

reminds me of a child waiting for their birthday party or a

Christmas celebration and all the gifts they will receive.

They wake up every day prior to the big day enthusiastic

because they expect good things. Start practicing being

excited with childlike faith as you wake up daily. Ask

God if this is the day for your blessing, breakthrough, or

healing, etc. "Daddy God, is today the day?" Jump up and down if that helps. Start praising and thanking God for what He will do.

2. Thought for the Week... Love

Walk in His love. What can you do to walk in His love? You can tell people how much they mean to you. Write letters of love and affection. You can tell them how much God loves them and show them what the word says about His love for them. Think about what you can do. Do something loving every day this week.

3. Thought for the Week... Praise and Worship

God deserves our praise and worship, but this is something God also uses to benefit us. As we worship and praise God, we draw closer to Him and we are uplifted and healed. When you wake, thank God for what you have and for who He is. Start your day with praise music and sing along.

Every day I will bless you, And I will praise your name forever and ever. Great is the Lord, and greatly to be praised; And His greatness is unsearchable. (Psalm 145:2-3 NKJV)

4. Thought for the Week... Dream

What are your deepest dreams and desires? Pray and ask God if they are beneficial; if not, ask Him to give you dreams that are better suited for you. Write them down and ponder over them; you must be willing to pay the price and do the work. It is time to start working on your dream. What do you need to do? Write a plan, and some steps to take. Start working your plan this week; you will be one step closer to your dreams. Reward yourself after you complete some steps. Examples: Have an ice cream, buy a nice pair of shoes, do something fun with a friend, etc. Make the reward fit the amount of work you put in. Little work, little reward, more work, bigger reward. Learn how to reward and encourage yourself and become your number one cheerleader. If you can get a friend to encourage you and keep you accountable, that would also help, but do not count on it. Count on yourself and God. You've got this!

5. Thought for the Week... Empower

Empower others with your speech. Speak edifying, uplifting words to others. Remember, God's word tells us we create and destroy with our tongues. We have what we speak. With that in mind, I challenge you to speak only positive words this week. Speak good things to your family and friends. Even if they are not walking as they should be. Declare that they will do good. If you get discouraged and you say something negative, correct yourself and say something positive. "You are important to God and to me." "Things will get better for you. I will keep you in prayer." "You are a great man of God! You will accomplish good things for God." "God loves you and so do I."

6. Thought for the Week… Advance

It is time to advance. What makes you do the things you keep doing? What are your beliefs and your motivations (your wants and your needs) and are they helping you to move forward or do they keep you going in circles? We get all kinds of ideas and we try various solutions to get what we want. Many times, we find it does not work. Have you sought out God's wisdom? God has said in His word we are to ask Him to guide us. Many of us have taken challenges; take the God challenge. Get deep into his word. Pray and ask God what He would have you do and see what happens. If God is speaking to you, it should line up with the word of God. If it does not line up, it may be contrary to His will for you. Seek out godly counsel from trusted leaders to help confirm what you feel God is saying to you.

Prayer:

God, help me to get rid of any mindsets, traditions, or habits that are counterproductive to my prosperity.

Renew my mind with your truths and your ways. Teach

me and show me what I should do. Refresh and empower

me, God. In Jesus' name, I ask you let it be so.

7. Thought for the Week... Pray

The Bible tells us we are to pray without ceasing. Try it

this week. Pray when you arise and when you go to sleep,

pray when you wash dishes, clean the house, shower,

drive, go for a walk, etc. Pray for people as you drive by

them and you sense that they are lost, hurting, or in need

of something. If you are in danger, pray a quick "God

help" prayer. You do not have to pray out loud. You can

pray in your head, because God hears your thoughts.

8. Thought for the Week... Blessing

Find a way to be a blessing to at least one person a day.

Make a list of seven people you know who are hurting or

in need who could use a blessing. Write down some ideas

of things you can do for them. Here are some examples:

Call people who are hurting or ill and pray for them. You can tell someone why you admire them or why they are special to you. Better yet, put it in a card or letter so they can read it over and over again. They may need a listening ear, or a ride. Perhaps someone is short on cash and you can bless them with a little money, or you can buy them something they really need. A single parent may appreciate a babysitter so they can have some free time and be refreshed. Invite someone over for dinner and a funny movie. Remember, God said that laughter brings healing, so share some laughter with someone.

9. Thought for the Week... Hope

Build a hope memorial. I feel like God wants me to encourage you to trust Him. People need hope. A good way to have hope is when we look back and can see what God has done in the past for us and for others. This builds our faith and hope for better things to come. I have seen God move in miraculous ways over and over again for me, my family, friends, and acquaintances. He can do it for you too. Build a memorial similar to what they did in biblical times. Get a special journal and write down how God has moved, saved, and healed you and others in the past. If you cannot think of anything, ask your friends or family for some moves of God in their lives, or pull some out of the Bible. The parting of the Red Sea is a great one. Place the book where you can see it and read it whenever you need to be encouraged. You can also get a picture frame and draw a cross on a sheet of paper. Then write the different things you have seen God do in the past. Place the picture in the frame and put it where you can see it.

10. Thought for the Week... Mighty

We may be shaken but we will not fall if we prepare, for we are mighty in Him. Self-analysis is a vital part of personal growth and strength. Self-observation will show you the areas that need work. What causes you to get shaken? These may be your areas of doubt, anger, or fear. Just as it is good to know our strengths and giftings, we should also know the areas where we are weak. What are your weak areas? What are your triggers? Write them down so that you can make a plan to deal with them. What can you do to heal, protect, and strengthen yourself? Perhaps you can take some classes, read some self-help books, see a life coach, pastor, or counselor to help you sort everything out. Find scriptures that apply and write them down and say them daily. Ex: For God has not given us a spirit of fear, but of power and of love and of a sound mind. (2 Timothy 1:7 NKJV)

11. Thought for the Week... God

Think about who God is to you. How do you view God? Is He strong, all knowing, loving, forgiving, and mighty, or is God angry, harsh and limited in your eyes? Do you really believe that God loves you just as you are, or do you find yourself thinking you have to meet certain conditions for Him to love you? Is God everything to you? Do you include Him fully in your life or does He occupy just a small portion of your life? Do you put God in a corner and only include Him when you need Him or when it is convenient? Are you open and honest with God, or do you try to pretend and hide things from him? This week, ask God to clarify who He really is and where He should be in your life.

Prayer:

God, forgive me if I have limited you in my beliefs and in my life. Help me to really know you. Enlarge my mind and heart to encompass all that you are. God, heal any broken places in me and create in me the capacity to receive your love and to love you fully in return. In Jesus' name I ask.

12. Thought for the Week… Happy

Take time to be joyful and make yourself happy. God tells us we are to enjoy the fruit of our labor. He has come to give us joy and an abundant life. As we spend more time with God, we should be filling up on peace and joy. Think of fun things to do. Write them down and make time for some of them this week.

The humble also shall increase their joy in the Lord, And the poor among men shall rejoice In the Holy One of Israel. (Isaiah 29:19 NKJV)

The thief does not come except to steal, and to kill, and to destroy. I have come that they may have life, and that they may have it more abundantly. (John 10:10 NKJV)

Peace I leave with you, my peace I give to you; not as the world gives do I give to you. Let not your heart be troubled, neither let it be afraid. (John 14:27 NKJV)

13. Thought for the Week... Journal

Buy a nice journal and a good pen and write in it daily. Write out your thoughts and feelings. What is on your mind or heart today? Write about it. As you study the word, write down any thoughts or impressions you get while reading. If you are sad or hurting, write about this too. This is where some of my best writing comes from, the time I spend with God, and the times when I feel the most broken.

14. Thought for the week... Fast

There are times when we must fast, according to the Bible. There are also many benefits to fasting. Here are a few benefits. We draw closer to God, we gain strength and clarity, we can pray for others with more power, we gain victory, deliverance is attained for us and others, and many more people are saved. There are different ways in which you can fast. You can do a full fast, have nothing but juices, fast half-day, fast a meal a day, or give up something you really like to eat. Do it according to what your health can handle. You can ask God what you should fast. During your fast, spend a lot of time in prayer and in the word. Journal your results.

Then the disciples came to Jesus privately and said, "Why could we not cast it out?" So Jesus said to them, "Because of your unbelief; for assuredly, I say to you, if you have faith as a mustard seed, you will say to this mountain, 'Move from here to there,' and it will move; and nothing will be impossible for you. However, this kind does not go out except by prayer and fasting." (Matthew 17:19-21 NKJV)

15. Thought for the Week… Believe

Live each day as if you really believe God's promises to you. If God gave you a promise and you believe Him, you would move in that belief and do your part to attain what God has told you. Write down what you believe God has told you and what you should be doing. If you have not been given any promises, pray and then look in the Bible and pick out a few. Write them out and review and pray over them regularly. An example would be if you believe God told you that you will be a teacher, a musician, or a writer. You should start your research and start taking the appropriate classes.

God tells us in his word that we are His children and we have his favor. How would a favored godly child act? They would act similarly to their father. Loving, forgiving, and patient. They would ask for things and expect them. This week ask your heavenly father for something and act like you believe you have His favor and love. Do your best to act like his obedient loving child. We will never be perfect, but when we fail, we ask God to forgive us and we try again. God is faithful; if He said a thing, it will come to pass. We can count on it. This week I want you to act like you really believe. Try stepping out and go for it. Remember, some things take time, but you are planting the seed.

Trust in the Lord with all your heart, And lean not on
your own understanding; In all your ways acknowledge
Him, And He shall direct your paths. (Proverbs 3:5-6
NKJV)

Opportunities

One year I had several doors open at once. I had a story
published and I had a few publishers interested in a book
proposal for a book I was writing. I met Lee Ann Thieman at a
writers' conference. She is an awesome woman of God. She read
some of my material and said she really liked it. She gave me a
hug and she said that she saw ministry all over me. She was right.
I had to set the book aside when I got back to California because
I was immediately launched into ministry working with women,
leaders, and women in shelters. That and other circumstances
caused me to push the book aside. When I think about it, I am a
little sad about letting some great opportunities slip buy. I believe

with some hard work and God's blessings; new doors will open for me. We all have dreams, but many times we have to lay them aside. Days slip by and we may forget our dreams. I would not want that for you. I want to encourage you to not give up on your aspirations. Push yourself and help others attain their dreams, too.

My Prayer for You

May your lips speak new words,

May you have new sight and new vision,

May you dream big dreams,

May you dare to do new things,

to travel to new places,

to get out of your comfort zone,

to run hard after the things of God.

May you search deep within yourself

until you uncover the secret place

deep within you that has kept

your dreams locked up tight.

And may you find God's key that

unlocks them and sets them free,

So that you will be filled

with so much joy…

That God places a new song in your heart

that you must sing...

and live out.

May God bless you in mighty ways. May you feel His presence

and hear His voice. May God guide you into some glorious years

of attaining all your dreams and goals!

In Jesus' name I ask.

Blessings and love,

Ruby

About the Poet / Author

 Ruby Heaton has an Associate Degree in Biblical Studies and an Associate Degree in general studies. She is a CLASS Communicator and a Life Coach. She led women's ministry, taught children's and adult Bible studies, taught at Women's shelters and at various churches, led prayer groups, and built up leaders. She has written in church website blogs and bulletins, and had a story published in *Moments of Grace*. She has been involved in ministries assisting pastors and is a co-founder of the Destiny Defender Ministries, and The Butterfly Ministries. She has had speaking engagements at churches, women's retreats, and women's shelters.

Website: www.RubyHeaton.com

Study Guidelines

1. You can meet with one friend or a few friends. You can meet on Zoom or another online platform, in person at a coffee shop, or in a home.

2. Decide on a day and time to meet. Set a reading plan, one chapter or a section. You can adapt it as necessary if you need more time to cover certain sections. You can decide as a group if you want to start doing the weekly challenges in Chapter 12 now or at the end of the study. Some people may not be able to do both at the same time.

3. Here are a few ideas. A.) Have water, juice, coffee, dessert, or fruit. B.) Set up a sign-up sheet for everyone to take turns bringing a desert and juice. C.) Or keep it really simple: have everyone bring their own water, juice, or coffee.

4. Have one person lead; there has to be someone who keeps things on track. Let everyone who wants to share have a chance to talk. Do not embarrass anyone, but

keep them on track. Say, "Let's stay on the topic." You may need to set a time limit if you have someone who is long-winded.

5. If someone did not do the study, encourage them to attend anyhow. Tell them that they will still get a lot out of listening and being with the group. You can have people take turns reading a few pages out loud or the whole chapter. Maybe a few people may want to read something that impressed them. Tailor the study in a way that suits your group.

6. Tell the group that whatever is shared needs to remain confidential. It should not be shared even with a spouse.

7. The leader should open in prayer.

    Prayer:

    God, meet us and lead this study. You know what needs to be said, who is hurting, and who needs healing and encouragement. God, meet all our needs. Help us be in unity and encourage one another. In Jesus' name. Amen.

God said to ask Him and he would answer and teach us. *Call unto me, and I will answer thee, and show thee great and mighty things, which thou knowest not. (Jeremiah 33:3 KJV)*

8. Have paper or index cards and pens on hand. At the end of your study, pass them out. Ask everyone to share a prayer request and write them down so you can remember to pray for them throughout the week.

Chapter 1 – Storms and Valleys

1. Read James 1:2-4, Proverbs 1:27, and Psalm 23:3-4 on pages12 and 18. What is God telling us about trials, storms, and valleys?

2. Think back on trials you have encountered. What was your worst trial and what effects did it have on you and those around you? Example: growth, knowledge gained, changes that took place due to the trial?

3. Did you make mistakes or act in ways you shouldn't have? Do you wish you would have handled a situation differently? If yes, how?

4. What are your greatest insights or lessons learned from your trials?

5. What advice would you give others going through various trials?

Chapter 2 – Deep Calls unto Deep

God has been calling and speaking to men and women since Genesis. God spoke to Abraham (Genesis 12:1-3), Hagar Sarah's maid (Genesis 21:17-18), Mosses (Exodus 19:3), and Paul on the road to Damascus (Acts 9). 1Peter 5:10 says that God called us to His eternal glory by Christ Jesus. Men who wanted to inquire of God for direction or knowledge went to Seers (1 Samuel 9:9). God has always communicated with man.

1. Read 1 Corinthians 1:23-24. It refers to those that are called. What does "Christ is the power of God and the wisdom of God" to those who are called mean to you?

2. Have you ever felt that God was calling you or talking to you? What did you hear Him say?

3. Were you ever led or pushed in a certain direction to do something or call someone?

4. Have situations ever lined up as if someone was orchestrating events on your behalf? Explain what took place?

5. Do you know what your calling is or what your spiritual giftings are? Your gifts line up with what your destiny is or what you called to do. You can also ask friends and family what they think your gifts are. There are tests you can take on line and many churches offer them. You can also try stepping into them and see what happens. If one doesn't work out, try another area. If you feel you are called to teach, volunteer to teach at church.

6. "For many are called but few are chosen." (Matthew 22:14 NKJV) What do you think this means?

Chapter 3 – Rise Up

1. Go over the last page in chapter 3, Power to Create. What positive words will you say?

2. What empowers you, where do you draw your strength from? What do you do to help you stay or feel strong?

3. Think back to times when you were overwhelmed. What helped you get back up? Did you call on someone? If so who?

4. We all do some type of self-talk. What do you tell yourself?

5. And he spake a Parable unto them to this end, that men ought always to pray, and not to faint; … (Luke 18:1 KJV) What does this Parable mean to you?

6. Hear me when I call, O God of my righteousness: thou hast enlarged me when I was in distress; have mercy upon me, and hear my prayer. (Psalms 4:1 NKJV) This was

David's prayer to God. What do you think David might be feeling? What is he saying?

7. Write out your own prayer asking God for help and reminding yourself how God has helped you in the past.

Chapter 4 – Self-Check

1. Go to the end of this chapter and find Foundation Self-Check. Then answer the questions in the action steps.

Chapter 5 – Changes

1. Work on the action steps at the end of this chapter.

2. You can talk about the changes that happen in a lifetime. Growing up, raising a family, growing old.

3. Read Romans 12:2, 1 Corinthians 13:10-12 and give your thoughts on these scriptures.

Chapter 6 – Revelations

1. Go over the questions to ponder at the end of this chapter.

2. What lie of the enemy did you believe? What exposed or crushed the lie? Write down any negative or fearful thoughts you still have. Find a scripture to come against it. Example: If you have fear. God calls fear a spirit and He says it is not from Him, which means it is a bad spirit and we must get rid of it. Use 2 Timothy 1:7 and change it. Say: God did not give me a spirit of fear. God gave me power, love, and a sound mind. Fear I cast you out of me now. In Jesus' name! I thank you God for giving me a sound mind and for filling me with your love, power, boldness and the Holy Spirit.

3. Do you have any regrets that you can share? Pray for one another for release and healing.

4. God reveals many things to us if we ask and we search in his word. Read Deuteronomy 29:29, Jeremiah 33:3, Daniel 2:22, Isaiah 45:3, Amos 3:7. Write your thoughts on these scriptures.

Chapter 7 - New Seasons

1. Do the action steps at the end of the chapter.

2. Read Ecclesiastes 3-8. What does this mean to you?

3. What season did you just come out of and how did it affect you?

4. What season are you currently in?

Chapter 8 – Truths

1. How do you feel about the truth?

2. Can you handle the truth?

3. Do you believe it is always best to tell the truth?

4. (Numbers 23:19 NKJV) *God is not a man, that he should lie, nor a son of man, that he should repent. Has He said, and will He not do? Or has He spoken, and will He not make it good?*

   How does this truth make you feel and why?

Chapter 9 - This Crazy Faith Which Hopes Against All Odds

1. What does your faith look like?

2. Do you believe everything in the Bible? What do you doubt or struggle with? We all doubt at some point. The father in the verse below wanted to believe. We too can ask God to help us in an area where we struggle with full belief.

   Immediately the father of the child cried out and said with tears, "Lord, I believe; help my unbelief. (Mark 9:24 NKJV)

3. Has God given your promises? What are they? How long have you been waiting for your promise? Have you done your part?

4. Have you experienced any of God's miracles?

Chapter 10 – Life is Fragile-Handle with Love

1. What are your thoughts on love?

2. How do you handle love? Are you open, reserved, hurt and operating behind a wall?

3. What kind of home did you grow up in? Was it loving or was love withheld? Was love conditional? Did you have to perform to get love?

4. Read 1 Corinthians 13 to see what God says about love. Write in your own words what you think God is saying.

5. Verses 4-8 tells us specifically what love should look like or how it behaves. Write a numbered list of the attributes. Put them on an index card and place them where you can see them regularly.

6. Most of us have not experienced God's type of love. If love is a problem for. you may benefit from seeing a counselor and exploring solutions.

Prayer:

God, we come to you for healing. You know what each one of us has been through, so you know what we need. Heal our confused hearts, our battered broken hearts, and our neglected love-starved hearts. God teach us how to love as you love.

Chapter 11 - Prayer

1. Work on the action steps for plans and goals at the end of this chapter.

2. What are your thoughts and experience on prayer?

3. What does your prayer life look like?

Chapter 12 – Thoughts for the week

1. Go to chapter 12 and work on one topic at a time. If you decide you want more time for a topic feel free to change the time frame. There is no rush. You should continue to meet live or on online so that you can encourage one another and share your progress.

2. Continue to pray for one another. Decide how you will work this out. Everyone needs prayer partners. It makes life easier knowing there are people who care about your needs and struggles. Plus, there is more power when two or more gather to pray.

> *"For where two or three are gathered together in my name, I am there in the midst of them."*
> *(Matthew 18:20 NKJV)*

Visit my website to read more of my writing or to contact me.

You can also sign up for my email and get information about

new books, products, and contest.

Website: www.RubyHeaton.com

<u>Notes…</u>

Made in the USA
Monee, IL
19 February 2021